A Place for Starr

A Story of Hope for Children Experiencing Family Violence

By Howard Schor

Illustrated by Mary Kilpatrick

KIDSRIGHTS®

Text © 2002 by Howard Schor

Illustrations © 2002 by Mary Kilpatrick

Published by KIDSRIGHTS®, an imprint of JIST Life, LLC
8902 Otis Avenue
Indianapolis, IN 46216-1033

Editors: Becca York and Sandy Cameron
Cover and Interior Designer: Trudy Coler
Proofreader: Jeanne Clark

Printed in Canada

06 05 04 03 02   9 8 7 6 5 4 3 2 1

ISBN 1-55864-082-7

Dedication

This book is dedicated to all of our brave children.

Acknowledgment

A very special thanks to Sanctuary For Families.

My name is Starr.
I have a story to tell.

It ends up like heaven,
But it starts off like hell.

A world falls apart
Where there is abuse.

When a man hits his family,
There can be no excuse.

If it's your father or
A friend who is violent,

You have to speak up.
You can't afford to be silent.

Some people say
My dad has no soul,

But it's nothing like that.
He's just out of control.

People say Mom is weak,
But to me she is strong.

She does what she has to
To protect us from wrong.

I have so much to share.
Our story starts off with woes

Of me, Mom, and Tyler,
And here's how it goes.

Tyler and I hide
Under the bed

To keep us safe
From getting hit in the head.

Mom tries to tiptoe
To keep peace with Dad,

But it never works
'Cause he always gets mad.

We all try to calm him,
But we always get blamed.

He makes us feel small.
We're all so ashamed.

He picks up a strap
Or a brush or his fist.

He yells about something,
Like the dinner he missed,

And says, "Don't complain
Or I'll twist off your wrist."

Then he gets louder
And it gets really bad.

There's no place to hide
From a man who goes mad.

And just when I think
There will never be peace,

There's a knock on the door.
Someone called the police.

They calm down my dad.
Soon the fighting is done.

They say, "Think of your daughter
And remember your son."

If this happens again,
We must call 9-1-1.

So after he's hurt us
With punches and slurs,

The strangest of wonders
Then often occurs.

He promises goodness.
He'll cry and he'll plead

Until Mommy forgives him
For making her bleed.

I confess to my mom
Just how sorry I feel.

I know it's my fault
Dad acts like a heel.

Mom strokes my head
As she sings me a song.

Then she assures me
I have done nothing wrong,

"Dad is responsible
For the life that he makes.

You can't blame yourself
For the actions he takes."

Then all is okay
For a week or so,

But Dad's like a volcano,
Always ready to blow.

We all talk in whispers.
My home's full of gloom.

But, of course, we say something
That makes him go, "Boom!"

And that's how we wind up
In the emergency room.

During the week
When I go to school,

I hide all my bruises.
I wanna be cool.

My teacher is troubled.
She says, "What is that?"

I say, "Oh, it's nothing.
I slipped on a mat."

I hate to go home
Down that long, lonesome road.

Oh, how many times
Have I watched him explode?

But tonight all has changed
And I won't shed a tear.

Mom hands me a suitcase
And says, "We're all outta here!"

We fly down the stairs,
Not a minute to lose.

We're so filled with fear,
But it's freedom we choose.

And we leave, oh, so quickly
We forget Tyler's shoes.

Where shall we go?
Who shall we see?

Is this how it feels
To be finally free?

The big city's so wild.
People run helter-skelter,

But Mom says there's safety
At a place called The Shelter.

We walk and we walk
'Til our muscles are sore.

Mom's shoulders are shaking
As the skies start to pour.

And just when we feel
We can't go anymore,

We arrive under a light
Before a giant new door.

Tyler is nervous.
He clings onto me.

Mom talks with the counselors
And the lawyers for free.

Soon they take Mom
To her new support group,

And we go to the playroom
To have sandwiches and soup.

With children like us,
We laugh and we play.

We draw pictures, make hats—
What a wonderful day!

Then our teacher, Miss Betty,
With a smile on her face,

Says, "Clean up and come over
To our magical place."

The circle holds magic
Because you can share

With people who'll listen
And who'll actually care.

I get up my courage
To say I feel sad.

With all that has happened,
I still love my dad.

Later we go to the
Home where we'll live

Thanks to these people
Who just want to give.

There we meet families
Just like our own

Who have left dads behind
To face the unknown.

It has been a long journey,
But it's just begun.

Today was a day
That was actually fun.

Now we're safe in our room.
Mom is brave, says, "We'll cope."

Tonight we can dream
Of a future with hope.

The Beginning